THE
MOTHER
ISLAND

A POETRY COLLECTION BY
JACINTH HOWARD

THE MOTHER ISLAND

A POETRY COLLECTION BY
JACINTH HOWARD

Advance Praise

"Jacinth Browne-Howard's poetry collection, *The Mother Island*, reveals an astute choice of word, image and metaphor that reflects her own peculiar insight and budding wisdom into the woman's everyday but also complex life experiences. In addition, this poet possesses a noticeably keen ear for the rhythm and meter that best enhance her themes and subject matter. A talented young poet."

— *Esther Phillips,*
Poet Laureate of Barbados

"In four orchestrated sections of *The Mother Island*, Jacinth Howard presents a rich compilation of poems in which she explores a wide range of themes related to motherhood, nature, love, the complexities of life, issues of womanhood. Some poems express the reverence one might feel when witnessing the "orange plumes / villainous smoke / rumbling earth" from an island volcano; others convey the awe that observation of animals in their natural habitats can bestir. Her use of figurative language is evocative, and her choice of metaphors conjure graphic images that linger long after reading. Howard's tone varies from elation to subdued self-assertion as she deftly navigates the thematic intricacies reflected in this, her first collection. She leaves us with eager expectation for future publications."

— *Hazel Simmons-McDonald,*
Professor Emerita, The University of the West Indies

The Mother Island
Copyright © 2023 by Jacinth Howard
All rights reserved.

Print ISBN 978-976-96420-0-3; Epub ISBN 978-976-96410-1-0

Published by Brown Bird Publishing

Author photos by Jannah Browne

Cover and book design by Tao Howard of Kainos Creative Studios Inc.
KainosCS.com

*I dedicate this work to my son, my light – Lucas
and my daughter, my smile – Adele
without whom I would not have acquired new
spectrum and strength to write and to mother.*

This work was born with you.

Author's Note

Thanks to the UNESCO Transcultura Programme and the European Unión for selecting parts of this work for reading and publication. Also, thank you for facilitating travel and the book's promotion at the Marché de la Poesie, Paris, June 2023.

Table of Contents

Acknowledgements 1

Sections

I

HURRICANE SEASON 2

II

WENCHCRAFT 22

III

ANIMAL TALES AND OUTINGS 50

IV

PARADISE 68

Notes 94

About the Author 96

Acknowledgements

I would like to thank God for seeing this work through from beginning to end.

I am grateful to Professor Jane Bryce for her honest, clear insight and her instrumental role as a reliable critic in this work.

Thanks to my husband Allan who sacrifices for my gifts and supports my every endeavour.

Thanks to my sister-in-law Julie who advocates for my work with her time, effort and heart.

Thanks to my parents, Frederick and Hannah Browne, particularly my mother who nurtured my writing since I was a child, my sisters Jannah and Janielle who act as my long-term sounding boards. Janielle, my true sister poet and storyteller – thank you.

Thanks to Kainos Creative Studios Inc. for facilitating the publication of this book and special thanks to Tao, my sister in arms, for your art and labour of love.

Thanks to Shaniqua Forde for her encouragement, her quiet investments and her big belief in this work and my ability from the inception.

Special thanks to the members of Writers' Ink and The Nucleus whose rich wells of love, validation, support and wisdom inspire me to continue writing. I am particularly grateful to Esther, Hazel and to Lafleur.

Thanks to my friends and family, to those who have always supported my aspirations and my creativity. Thanks to all of the leaders and peers who have spoken positively into my life and my career.

I could not do this without any of you. Thank you!

HURRICANE SEASON

*It's almost as if they're little islands in a sea of adult people
Who do not really care about them.*

- DOLACE MCLEAN -

*I am the mother,
dancing in the tempest.*

OYA

OYA

I used to think I had lost myself,
Engulfed in whistling gales.
Swept away, like hurricane come,
Windswept hair and waterworks,
Wild, chaotic rooms in greyscale,
Scattered leaves, torn newspaper debris
Waiting to be kissed by order:
Re-embraced by a familiar island girl,
Beneath the harmony of the sun.
A tiny wish sailing on the distant horizon.
Then in a single, silent moment,
I understood.
I looked her in the eye, held her still.
I rained with words, made music with deluges.
I inscribed it as law:
I am the mother, dancing in the tempest.
I am the daughter, harmonising with the torrent.
I am the woman, born of the storm.

A HEAD

At times
Her thoughts swivel
The opposite way.
She's always been a step ahead
Of the pack
A lone
Wolf
And suddenly,
She's dealt
A Joker
A statistic
In the middle
A digit
Reshuffled
By the hands of time
Trying not to fall behind
Instead
Keeping
A head
Only above water

PORCELAIN

Porcelain placed on a shelf.
Granny's best china
Chaste and certainly speech-less
Delightful eye catcher
Only heard in rebellious clattering
On unforgiving tiles below.
Body broken in with trained waists
Made up veneer of happiness
Hiding caged thoughts and loaded mouth
Perfection shattered open.
The bristles do the dirty work,
Capture each crystal shard of potential
Shifting them one by one to an obscure corner
Where miscellaneous items
Too uncooperative for display
Will at least be kept from catching attention
In a way that really leaves a mark.

THE SILENCED SISTER

You sit there, stained glass eyes:
Wide open windows,
Streak across your face, bloody crimson
Sealing in a world of truths
First, you can't get out,
Second, it will hurt each time
Third, no one will know
Fourth, it will stay that way.

Nobody's home though lights are on
You hope that silence would speak for itself
Tired solutions lie like used newspapers
In the corridors of your mind
Only his words publish these days
In your ear waves,
On the screen of your heart

Your heart is his,
At least it used to be.
Until he realised it wouldn't stop beating.
So, he wouldn't stop beating
Dragging Rapunzel by her rope of hair
Severing every escape route
Breaking your beauty inside and out
With love (on occasion) all throughout
So, you would never leave.

All jokes aside,
No language of laughter
Slave stifling in stitches, suppers, and service.
Talking with your hands
To mend shirts
To protect yourself

To wipe your face
To hold entrails in
To polish the children
To make up your face
For public display

The walls whisper twice to run
The bushes promise they can help
But all they do is run their mouths
To everybody else.
They don't know
The sternum crushing embraces
The butterfly kisses
The closet full of new faces
To cover the one he's distorted.

So you sit there, in the dragon's lair
Marked by the beast, eyes dull with fear
Waiting for the raptor's next sudden game
Hoping you won't break though porcelain.
Then he'll end with "I love you" again
What happens beyond this picket fence,
Is coached into smiles and dead silence
Before it's too late
Won't someone make statement?
Won't someone make testament?

A SONG IN ASYLUM

She is beyond help,
They said.
Hauling up howls
Involuntarily from a harrowed glottis
Hitting hollow walls like hardened ears
Ringing down the halls of the hospital.

After the tentacled cackler
Ripped the happy melody from her song
There was only the sound of silence.
Beneath the surface,
Emotion undulating, seizure the body
Bind and mum her, bedridden by fear
Strapped in misery, an incontinence of tears
Incoherent mumbles.

Sunlight would not cure the sallowness
No medication for this mania, they said
Shaking unqualified heads and fingers.
Quacks shoving potions of dissent
Pills of pragmatism, pity painkillers
Hallucinogens for happiness
Things get better when you cooperate
When you gi dem evuhting,
When you smile.
Sitting in the red roof house
Beside the fence,
The locked up room behind bars.

One day she would take it further.
She would laugh.
Notes that then ascend to liberal screams
She's crooning them into words

And they'll grow legs, do incredible runs.
Snatch safety up and hold it hostage.

Perhaps she would never sing again,
But this time, she would be heard.

UNDERMINING EDEN

They say it was a woman,
Who undermined Eden.
Performed the first trade of human bodies.
Permanently expelled from paradise:
For glowing, green eyes and power lust.
Still in effect post life sentence.
Despite the virgin's painful sacrifice
To redeem mankind,
Woman is still paying plenty.
Multiplied sorrow, responsibility
Believed to be brought on
As Lilithian penalty
All meeting at the midpoint
Of an acute angle cuing kicks in the gut:
Issuing broken, disappointed cries
Scarlet signals, Mother Nature arrives
An exclamation: single, red-lined test
An exhalation of babes fatherless, bereft
The howling effects of infantile hauntings,
Another miscarriage that nobody's counting.
Issuing too often one thing of beauty
A pair of green eyes
Witnessing everyone else's
Loveliness but her own.
Still, she will not risk another fall.
She won't complain, she's satisfied
She'll buy no more serpentine lies
Of becoming gods with open eyes
If it means being cast out again.

*Witnessing everyone else's
Loveliness but her own.*

UNDERMINING EDEN

HORSEMAN PASS BY

When I wake up
Is night fall
Somebody suck
Two breaths out
From under muh nose
In two minutes flat
Muh eyes was close
And duppy done climb in

Not even double breasted
Guard enough
Golden milk ain't give them
Life enough
Uriel flame burn
Hot enough
Horseman ride me
Long enough
'Til I wake up

When I wake up,
I wish that they would too.
I ain't ask a soul to pass by.
Wish they would pass back
And un-it-do
Wish they could pass back
And tek me too
For nothing is worse
Than having died
With muh two eyes wide open.

SILENT NIGHT

Sleep in heavenly peace.
A dream, for the weary mother.
Yet, twitchy eyes bright
Like fairy lights, are vital signs of living.
Shrieks splitting still December darkness
Ring softer than Cherub without his harp.
Wrapping up a year with loss
Is never on a holiday checklist.

Yet it's always nice to uptick occasions
When strangers stretch
Olive branches of kindness
Monetary goodness, scintillating scents
Olive oil for ear infections,
Coconut oil for good skin and hair,
Finances. Fragrances. Future investments.
Buying success for the baby from early.

The myrrh however,
Should be naughty listed,
Snatching baby's breath prematurely,
Soiling the fabric of a family who must now
Scotch tape paper hearts together,
After an unseen marksman points to where
X marks the spot for murder,
Herod's looming sword.
Overcast Golgotha,
A misshapen tree
A man broken to be King.
A death defying act:
Cancelled mortality.
Brought together hearts with treasure
Repealed the maps from death's reach.

Here lives:
X, a hero of a son.

And the mother?
Wailing at the foot of murder unmerited,
Carries on faithfully
Watches him die helplessly,
Waits at the grave hopefully,
Somehow must mother another.

A chilling tale,
Eggnog bitter to taste,
She wants the cup to pass.
Prayers wrapped around her tense neck
And fidgeting hands
Occupying them.
For empty hands and hearts
Welcome unbearable Winter:
Singing Silent Night over steady infant breaths
Off-key-la-las before sudden eclipse
Sighing over void mangers and vacant cradles
Until the empty tomb that makes her
Smile

Eggnog bitter to taste,
She wants the cup to pass.

SILENT NIGHT

THE GIVER

When a heart can find
For(give)ness
It yields its greatest offering
Is it a gift of loss or gain?
Is it escorted by joy or pain?
Is it passing the hurt again?
Or breaking the cycle.
That is determined alone
By the giver

SOU SOU

It's my hand at the meeting turn.
Life grants its dues,
Then I pay in with prayers,
And hold my breath.

Months groan by
As I wait in faith.
That all will come back
Rewarding consistency
Abrahamic sacrifice

Blessed be His name
Who gives and takes away.

Then one day,
Favour washes me in returns,
Lifts me by many hands
With old, gleaming wedding bands
Which put in more than they owed
Leaving me soaked in rain of release,
Showered in comforting response.

Is God turn to put in now?

*The bubbles won't last,
But his laughter will*

VAPOUR

VAPOUR

Tiny hands are raising
A microscope in the rain.
No sunbeams sear through,
But bubbles filter from the portal,
Gliding through bleak atmosphere.
Transient and clean.
Vanishing with each raindrop collision.
Liquid landmines bursting on his plastic poncho.
Baby boots turned inwards,
Like little ducks disorderly:
Parading in the puddles.
The bubbles won't last,
But his laughter will.
And so, we still smile
When it rains.

WENCHCRAFT

*Practising my art
Lets me uncover new knacks.
Enduring past my strength
Makes me advance in becoming.*

Generations weaved together tight
Hold my hand steady in community.

BROWN BASKET

BROWN BASKET

A hand me down
Worn, tanned fibres
Strong against my calloused grip
Generations weaved together tight
Hold my hand steady in community.

One night, malicious fingers cut the threads
Fabricate grudges through woven lies.
Scattered on the waters the tattered ties.
Sewing hatred: a harrowing craft
An unrelenting taskmaster.

Who will help me lift this load?
Bear the weight of my mothers?
Find the strands of my sisters?
Plaited up in our hair,
Knotted up in our belly,
We take detours at every urge
To harbour second-hand hatred.

We will weave our way through silent roads
We will find each other again
Tie our ends back together,
Loop our arms again,
Knit our string that comes down so long
From something old into something new
But always ours
We will heal our little brown basket.

QUICK STITCH

You've undone yourself,
Sitting under a Singer
Your feet fishing for a steady pedal
For a quick stitch
Your ear yearning for a locomotive hum
But the thimble tucked under
The coral checkered gingham
May have to bear the clumsy, impatient needling
For now.

You'd never think
That you, a descendent of Mbombo
Could not make magic material,
When Bumba unspooled the wispy clouds,
That prance above, from spittle.

You'd never think
That the tangled threads and jagged cotton strips
Amassed below, like a congregation of dust bunnies
Casually disbanding into the quaint, neighbouring foyer
Were tightly spooled strands and an evenly cut white square
Blanketing the bed together up to this morning
Carefully laid, ready to be made a masterpiece.

But perhaps carelessness worked better
For the perfectly pressed, off-white dress
Before you – mocking and modelling.
Perhaps a flawless frock is born of chaos.

The only ease right now is in knitting brows together.
You toss some manuals to disguise the bunnies,
Shielding failure, a small respite.

Ten thousand hours to master a craft,
You remind yourself,
Seven days if you're divine,
But for all your earnest, mortal efforts,
You simply don't have that kind of time.

POETIC INJUSTICE

Yes.
It was adulterous.
Guilty pleasures in other sources.
Temporarily.

Smooth surface of paper
Pallid, pristine, untouched
For far too long.
Now I remember:
Your crisp ears caught it all.
Your pages a bosom for fallen tears.
Every feeling meant something to you.
Each careful stroke on clear, straight, deliberate lines.
Yet I have forgotten the sweetness of your quiet demeanour.
The purity of your skin until I sully it with dark, lustrous, dripping stains.

Instead I have made do with whispering sweet nothings
Shouting them even.
To faithless lovers and careless audiences.
You would crumple if you knew what I've done with your words.
Warped them for crude communications.
Distorting all the art we've made together.

But

I am here again.
By force perhaps.
Aren't they all?
Sorry. Again.
For striking you unexpectedly.
After striking up disingenuous conversation.
Hurting you for my own good.
Release.

Leaving behind a well-decorated, empty apology
My selfish offering
In exchange for your service, submission, and loyalty.

THE MINSTREL

It was a mock-up
Offstage
He knew it wouldn't last
Tuning into manifestoes:
Dying young, living fast.
Rotating swastikas, torches and nooses
Yoked to worship of the past.
She knew it could not last.

It wilted early.
Of course, it did.
Beautiful, brown leaves,
Curling in the breeze.
Rotten mangoes,
Once full on the trees,
Lay sweet in the dark earth,
Still and squeezed.

Death follows him everywhere.

She dried with it
And not like potpourri.
Like clothes on the line,
Like strange fruit.
Living and hanging,
Between hot empty air,
Out on a limb for him
To give nothing in return but make believe.

She dried with it
And not like potpourri.

THE MINSTREL

PENS

If pens grant us positions of power,
I will right my problems myself.
If you point your quill, you can too.
A key to open sesame,
A pencil for Invigorating Quests,
A mic to raise your voice,
A spatula to stir up wonders,
Quietly write your name on eternity.
Magic will unfurl and fly,
If you're brave enough to wave your wand.

LIMERICK

Genius of note,
Derek Walcott wrote,
A world renowned play,
In less than three days.
How much time should I devote?

Among scattered toys
Scribble haphazard joys
Jot thoughts but rock-a-bye for more hours
Pen here and there but dream for the power
To write like he did, was it a ploy?

Was it because,
His ears were not abuzz
(With a colicky wail
By a baby so frail)
That he would someday know the sound of applause?

NIGHT STANDARD

Should she wake her husband again?
Sometimes she wishes that she could send
Another mother who could ably bend
Over backwards until her back hurts.
She sits in the darkness to ease the pain
Shifts baby over shoulder and hopes to stay sane
Too deep in, to turn back or lean on complaints.

It's duty to keep a whole household in check.
And if all else fails, at least mother knows best.
For all the hows and whys she lost herself
Are irrelevant in this milk sodden moment
When instead of milking reasons to shout
A sleepy child looks up at her, milky-white-mouthed
Pink lids half-closed, he's unconcerned about
Whether mothers need rest to run too.

INSOMNIA

My mother wakes me up this time
Replaced the alarm in my mind
Of squirming, screaming little neighbour,
Beginning since the pains of labour.
My eyes like crumpled plastic wrap,
The sunlight hits and strikes like tacks
A vital consciousness I lack,
Or maybe it's still there ... perhaps.
Overslept cannot apply,
When I've been up at least six times.
How sleepless nights have dragged me here,
By cruel means I am aware.
The laundry dragon must be slayed.
The light bill must somehow be paid.
The dishes will remain unbathed.
My first time fears someway allayed,
To care the babe for whom I've prayed.
Hours, minutes, seconds came.
Cleaved to themselves became the same.
My face is sunken, fatigue smeared
My soul is stagnant, cold and bare
The thoughts that drone on of despair
Arrested by my will to care.
A stale and listless empty stare
To face the day, and even dare
To scale the heights of Schedule Mount,
And make sure that each effort counts.

PERFORMANCES

There's rank of hurled insides
Sprawled across the floor
Tempting little feet to slip
And mouths to do some more

Kicks atop your head at night
Whimpers and small squeaks
Prepare yourself to say goodbye
To any kind of sleep

The scattered toys, the early drives
The two feet never right
The nimble fingers strike again
Break everything in sight

Say "never mind" to friends again
They just won't understand
That though you've worked for weeks
You can't have 'pickney' and a plan

You'll smile again say things are great
You'll lean upon your brawn
You've learned to catch your breath and live
The show: it must go on.

Prepare yourself to say goodbye
To any kind of sleep

PERFORMANCES

REMEMBER YOU

Promise me
That you will remember you.
In missed appointments,
Feeble memory,
Accidentally broken promises,
Frequent fumbling and failures,
In tiny human needs,
Remember yours too.
As you find a way to bargain with brilliance
Fix your job, fix your house, fix dinner
Fix your husband
Remember you need fixing too.
Forget your purse, forget the keys
Friends will forget you too
But promise me when all is said
You will remember you

IN MINIATURE

The most frightening
And curious thing
Is recognising
Your reflection
In this small being
Seeing all your ways
On full display
In miniature
Publicly hoping
You're coaxing them away
Yet secretly hoping
Some will stay

THE LOOKING GLASS

I watch her close wooden doors in her face.
Hiding, enveloped in disguises.
When I find her,
I chase the trail of her titters,
Follow her leap through the vestibule,
Pursue her climb up to the vanity mirror.
Where she can really see.
Each time, the oblong frame marks a new increment.
She scales up before my eyes.
Each time, it takes less effort
To prise herself and rise to the occasion.

At first, I saw my stubborn pout
Determined, russet eyes
Robust dark skin.
Followed up by my impatient stewps
My refusals of equivalents between black and evil,
My inquiring mind on her mouth,
Then my laughter ringing.

I fear growing old.
And though my vivacious heart
Shines through in her life,
I resist the urge to live on in her.
It is not what good mothers do.
Still, she is a portrait of the artist not the sitter.
And I will do anything to ensure that
She sees beauty in the glass
And disavows every corrupt lie behind it.

POUIS AND AUTOCRACY

An empire,
Tended by fear,
Will never produce,
Healthy, loving citizens.
Icy, imperial thumbs,
Plucking up bright flowers by the neck,
Along with the weeds,
Will never foster flourishing results.
Water the seedlings with respect,
Cover them with encouraging mulch,
Expose them to yellow beams of knowledge,
Gaze at them with tenderness and watch them grow delightfully.
Your green thumb will show in the beauty of the blossoms
Express poui flush will teach you love.

One day, I cut it all off.
To start over again.

HAIRSTORY

HAIRSTORY

Flying hair
Telephone wire kind
Just like the church mothers'
Synthetic and tight.
Flooding our cathedral,
Fluffy and flying.
Lionesque and bobbing.

My first flying hair was hay-yellow
Adorned in independence of adulthood
Linking me to the elders
Who taught me to pray, to war,
To thunder my sole against the ground
Sound my will out loud
Always present, always proud
Of where I come from.

Flying hair,
Crowned upon
My mongoose tinted plumes
Tamed beneath my mother's
Practiced fingers, inscribing 'cascado'
Protective styling, coated with blue magic
Saturday evening bread: formula,
for luscious locs to last and last.

One day, I cut it all off.
To start over again.
But that... is a different story.

RUSTIC CHARM

Women of war,
Far out beyond idyllic hills,
Wide open cane fields,
Wanting more than outdoor hearths for hunger,
And coteries where cuts and splinters are common.
Healers they're called:
Wanting more than inherited herbal solutions,
Fitting fragile bones into natural spaces,
Stirring cornmeal for hungry faces
Giving broken men some places
Of comfort.
Rest, for wooden cases.
Women whose knees are bruised,
Whose fingers are calloused,
Branches and cracks walk across her soles.
Perhaps she has no room to dream,
Like Isis, room for nurturing cycles
Of thriving and perishing.
Their wombs make room for generations.
Their hands set sacrifices adrift on water,
They spin webs and threads, mending, altering
Weave ebbs and flows; rises, falls,
Her able hands have held it all.
Perhaps someone sees her solitary work,
And kindly wishes:
Mothers may your casualties be few.

MUTINY

Sometimes,
The most peaceable living,
Can only take place,
At a distance.
Adrift in a row boat, with a sleeping toddler
And clothes clinging to her
Burdened back and knotted belly.
Facing salt spray of uncertainty
Garinagu hair straggled by yearly resistance.
Still, refusing to elevate that white burgee,
A desperate S.O.S., a banner of begging,
For sponsored but uncomfortable living.
For what are de-kinked, coiffed hair
And stirrup ballroom dresses,
Behind bars of heavy handed laws?
There'll never be rest in embracing
The concrete decision to disagree
Or the powdered stiff upper lip
At the cul-de-sac community
Clucking about
Isolation
When what she signed up for was
Independence.
She'll take the oars into her own hands.
Even a rudderless canoe in open water
Will go somewhere.
Destination unsure,
Still she can hone her own craft,
Until she gets far,
And finding herself
Is destination enough
For now.

COMMUNICATION

Funny how we learn to talk
As infants
Then suddenly forget
How to construct conversation
As adults

RETURN ADDRESS

Over time I've realised that
I can't go home anymore.
Home is a place,
Where you find shelter.
Home is a space,
Where bad weather,
Will not whittle away,
Your resolve.
Or while away,
Your time.
Or dissolve
Who or what you are.
Home is a space in the head.
A memory changing,
A room re-arranging,
A temporary thing,
A love unfettered and escaped
With no return address.

FREE SPEECH

But this is who I've always been.
Have you not paid notice?
Marooned and littoral.
Still, turbulent seas of opinion,
Could not drown out the storm inside,
Or dam the flow of conviction in my eyes
Or stem the fixed perspective in my mouth.
I'm washed ashore with certainty,
That I can rebuild anywhere
For the hearth inside me is enough.
Winds of change, have not changed me
They've only brought me
Home.

I'm washed ashore with certainty,
That I can rebuild anywhere

FREE SPEECH

ANIMAL TALES AND OUTINGS

III

If I planted myself deep
And tried to grow within the loam
Could ethereal earth connection leap
Then fly to take me home?

*People point fingers anywhere
But at themselves.*

INSTINCT

INSTINCT

People point fingers anywhere
But at themselves.
But you point pistol to your chest.
For accountability
Jasmine aromas on your wrists for deflecting
But guilt like fish scent all over you.
Polite, upturned smile to welcome
But hidden claws in each paw ready to scar
If any dare pet your young.
And they smilingly ask for permission.
Still you brace,
Adrenaline veiled,
Snarl disguised,
Muscles tensed,
Untrusting eyes.
Their steady hand on revolver keeps the worst at bay
But you are equipped to kill if it came to it.

BLACK DOG

How me supposed to feel?
Me one child spent
Feel up like dolla bread
Sit down up at Red Roof
Wagging she head
Gone half past crazy
They said
Me still nah buy it.

How me supposed to feel?
Seeing she torment
Watching she nod
She eyes dem shot up
And full of blood
Hope run down she face
Demoralized flood
Roll over she cheekbone levees.

How me supposed to feel?
Detective hat on
Still looking for clues
Sniffing around
Like me name Scooby Doo
Me one child spent
And me want to know who
Got she howling and bent
Like Magadog self
Tail between her legs.

Tho' me dog-tired,
Ah go defeat d devil.
Done with bacchanalian barking
Up the wrong zaboca tree

They really feel that I sky-larking
Me go hound hell to save the child
Dem ah find out is more than old talking
That a mother's wrath is a scourge.

SPIRITED STALLION

Somewhere along you feared the horses.
Majestic steeds with graceful manes
Terrifying whinnies, rumbling hooves
Cracking whips, throttling speeds
That is how you remember them.

Somehow your child tames the wild.
All you needed was gentleness.
The beast in the corral was always waiting
Genially prepped just for befriending.

But your hands only knew cruelty
Made a total enemy
Of a creature born to be an ally.

When you learn that liberty comes
With an unlatching of the gate,
A forgoing of the second thought,
A release of confessions on the backs of wood doves,
A tightening of trust in place of the reins,
A drawing back of the hand when temptation hits,
He will bolt through the door, gallop wildly,
Vanish beyond the trees.

But the sweet creature will always return
To a place where he learns love.

Somehow your child tames the wild.
All you needed was gentleness.

SPIRITED STALLION

TERRAPIN

Imagine quick, you, working twice as hard,
To become half of who you were, discard
The past, to chase youth, springing on hare's fleet,
While you are grinding worn and mimsy teeth.
Craned neck, optics swallowed by taloned feet,
Sluggish, steady, spidering, obsolete.

Still, the rabbit races away, soft and small,
Sometimes slipping, you worry he will fall.
Skipping the trap of your cold blooded 'no',
He will not hold up because you say so.
Dragging the world on your shoulders, you shout,
But only weak breaths collapse from your mouth.

You know how this goes, leatherback refined,
The clock ticks against you, stifles your time.
No pause, can't think, there's no room to linger.
You're cursed with age, he's slid through your fingers.
No pause, can't think, how much time has elapsed?
You continue to miss with each imprecise grasp.

Strong and sturdy but inside scared to death,
Sells a serene façade with bated breath,
Ancient mariner, well meditated,
Built home in yourself, you cultivated,
Perfection. a tight, stern city afloat,
A well-run, hand crafted, pine scented boat.

And all for nothing when it all shatters
A broken egg, everything scattered
Smashed, foregrounded by your outgribing

Impossible to catch, tiny varmint
When he's plunging straight down the rabbit hole
Again.

A PORKER

Today your limbs get filthy in the mud
You're grumbling and grunting unintelligibly
Your face is buried in the overflowing trough
You do not care.
Your snout shivers at the stench on your spotted skin
You roll on your back and cannot get up again
It is one of those giving up days.
Perhaps if you were ceramic, they would feed you money.
Beautiful and untouched but otherwise useless.
But today, you are dirty.
Your teats are yanked in several directions,
A few pounds would be nice to lose,
But today you are grateful for utility.

MINDING CATTLE

When my father was small,
The dawn transported him
To clear fields where his cattle wandered.
It taught him responsibility.
My son inherited this wonder of cows
When his eyes open, he takes me to watch them.
Differently, I've no more tolerance for cowing.
Motor mouths, loud and sonorous
Singing the same bovine tunes
Day in, day out
Painting the same blues
Grinding away the most
At what they know least
Wielding tradition
Offering cud
Chewed many times over
The way it's supposed to be
Changing the oil
Only when it suits them,
And inconveniences you.
Attempting to woo your child away
With sweet, coddling moos
And watery eyes.
But the older he grows,
He chooses the window, over the road,
As a vantage point to watch them
For he is learning that minding cattle
Incurs responsibility.

THE DESERT

There must be an oasis
To stop prey from purposelessly running
Antelope legged,
Stepping into outer
Darkness.
Full milky mooned, arctic atmosphere,
Dry dust clumsily aiming at the eyes by the handful
Breath
Ragged and laboured
Any exchange of air
Means promise
Or else,
Carcass.
Worse yet:
Is one eye open, one shut.
Limbo, purgatory,
Wandering is no way to live.
If you will not hasten and choose to die
You must swallow and believe
That the light isn't out here
In the black desert air,
But in you.
Understand magic.
Miracles aren't always made overnight.
For the rocks won't bleed
Until you make them.
Until the water can run from your belly.

*Limbo, purgatory,
Wandering is no way to live.*

THE DESERT

METEORITE

If you plan to go out,
Do it like a meteorite.
If you must fade to darkness
First set yourself alight
There's not a lot of time here
There's nothing guaranteed
So, if you'll hit the ground below
Collide at rocket speed
Kill all the birds with one swoop
You're more than just a stone
Skip straight across the sea
And if you must, ripple alone
You're tougher still, and skyward now
You're soaring with a pelt
And though you'll hit the ground below
Your meaning will be felt
Reverberating, resonating
Snatch up your purpose fast
And going out just do your best
To strike the hardest
Last.

THE HIND

In the middle of the hesitancy
He is spurring your steps forward
In the mire of uncertainty
His calloused hands are displacing doubt
Refilling the trough with confidence in Him.
Constructed with bone like iron
Standing steadily alone
The match stick legs are gaining strength.
Walking in stride
With the One who made them.
He has witnessed every cinematic event.
He has marked the length of your footstep
He has broken onto every broken path
He has peered through the lens of your doe heart
He has trod every instance, every part
Of the journey before you.
The panorama of fields, shades, slips, hikes, dips
Contour His irises
He knows what it takes
Sure, that He's made you
Strong enough to make it.

*Beautiful at your lightest,
shining at your darkest.*

WATERCOLOUR

WATERCOLOUR

The first time you articulated
Transparent, fluid bodies
You ambled between 'wadur' and 'wata'

The first time you had a wash day
You clenched your teeth, resistant
As your mother's earthy ancestors did
And sprung from the basin
Hair water slicked
Like your father's pale forefathers did

The first time you embraced salty waves
The sun kissed you back
Made you olive
Beautiful at your lightest, shining at your darkest.

When the time comes,
I hope that you will decide not to choose.
Like water you will not hold still
You will not be confined.
You will remember that though
We flow from different sources,
We will all meet together in the end.

I've shifted shape for generations
Each time I realise
The more that I attempt to grow
The more I reach the sky
I love the land, breathe in the herbs
Disperse them far and wide.
I'm home wherever I set my feet
And when I close my eyes
Embrace the divine deep within
And dream of paradise.

PARADISE

*Creole capital letters floating from the copier,
Some desire to be heard.*

DARKERS

DARKERS

Knee high neon boots,
Statement making peacock feathers,
Splaying from the shoulders,
Tribal beads weaved across the face,
Some desire to be seen.

Beyond vacationer sunglasses,
Placards standing browner than pumped fists,
Impervious afros scaling higher than injustice,
Creole capital letters floating from the copier,
Some desire to be heard.

Lithe fingers unpacking the heart,
Flying fish soaring past pigeonholes,
Beanstalk dreams piercing dense clouds,
Pocketed voices escaping through fissures,
Some desire to be understood.

A SMALL PLACE

Everybody wants to leave
Weh dem ah go?
Me nah know
What is out dey?
Me nah kay

Just to go way and come back
Fine for me
Just to see thing and admire that
Quench me nosey

I left once before, yes
But to go to another tiny place
Surrounded by a smidgen of water
Not a mobaton of people
Sand and salt air
And just a drop of happiness

What I want with being a statistic?
What I want without me people paranging?
What I want with living invisible?
Lonely Londoners all over again
What I want with doors in my face?
What I want with defending my race?
Everyday so that it wearies yuh

Chuh

I looking for something simple
I looking for something ample
Foreign far-aways are for sample
But not for living on

Not for me anyway
I good right here so
Thanks very much

OYA II

She is still guided by the wind
Along waterways
Hovering along undulant mountain ranges
Soaring beside the sun
Resigning beside the still ocean
Dwelling on the interlaced fingers of golden grains and blue
She will rest on any gem instilled in azure
She will nest in any space that finds itself untethered
Declares its hand unconnected
Finds its roots marine
Unseen,
Undivinable.
Wandering the water
But not lost.

OZ

What I want to do
Is trade this emerald city,
Is shuffle on some red flats,
Tap them together and open my eyes.
Open them to crimson on a green backdrop
Dancers and nativity plays
Salutes, tiny bows and well learned recitations
Rebounding round the room
With little peeps, cupped mouths and wide eyes
Highlighting errors, we would not notice otherwise.
I want chilly 4 a.m. air for nine dawns
Gusts through low lying stars of several shades and shapes.
A whiff of callaloo and a bush tea slightly burnt tongue.
Laughter carries, blanketing safety in pockets of people.
Bringing warmth to the darkness beneath the well-lit space.
People then become jesters for prizes.
Pumpkin soup at Christmas dinner, pan and parang
Dust bunnies escaping old curtains and hijacking your nose
Or is that the sharp smell of new mats?
Sorrel-red lips, Danish cookie pans without needle work,
9 p.m. city shopping.
Grandma's cheesecake and a new book.
Lyrics you're only allowed to hear
Strung in that particular order once a year
Malt, ham and a tiny piece of black cake
For the stomach's sake.
Oh, Toto are we in Kansas again?

MYTH MAKING

Boarded up in being,
Locked in the temporary
Complex
Building too much on one side
Ignoring the next
All collapsing to nought
Atlantis submerged
El Dorado hidden
Troy destroyed
All for nothing
Empires falling
The story repeating
Yet we go on
Reaching with our fingers
For myth
And catching mist

Building too much on one side
Ignoring the next

MYTH MAKING

ENTER THE PALACE

After Gerardo Polanco

of Quetzalcoatl,
Kingdom, torn and torched by conquest,
Nahua's flamboyant, poinsettia lips exquisite
Sealed tight, robbed of Baby's Breath
The serpent slithers in surreptitious circles,
Silhouetting – the cracked and yellowed,
Mould-eaten, uneven brick,
With sharp, evergreen turns; tiny verdant feathers erect
Edge to curve, balance to nature,
Spiral body slinking slow,
Sprawled across expanse of earth,
Ruins
On shrouded paths, dusted with gold,
Slipping from skins of camouflage sheath
Sun-bathed bronze
Mystic
Ceremonial.
When snakes could fly,
Borne up by myriads of coloured quills.
Creating calligraphy
On codex of wind.
Gilded one, undulating,
Decorated with an array of cowries,
Armour close set, bricks in a wall,
Carefully hand painted and patterned.
Each stroke, exercising palette back and forth,
Round and round, filling each space with pastel hues.
Divine one, dwell here,
Someday soon.
Dance upon this dais of death –
Arise from the smoky ashes.
And live.

OBSIDIAN - An Ode to Soufriere

Many pledge pro patria
But I fear the motherland
Her eyes aflame, her rattling cough
Creates the sand - obsidian

Her locs of emerald
Twine and twist
Unfurling through
The jungle's mist

Her children stretch
Their arms of green
In worship to her sky
Serene

But when she blows
Consumes the land
In hail and stones
Obsidian

Her praises sung
In rumbling Earth
Assails the darlings
She once birthed

Orange plumes
Creep cross the clear
Villainous smoke
Eats passive air

In selfish vengeance
Maiden's bite
And ash bathed spit
Collude with night

The sons of man
Once told to share
Are ousted -
Mere sojourners here

In poisoned water,
Green fields flat,
Dirt caked children,
Buildings black,

Broken cisterns,
Emptied banks,
Cryptic prophets,
Charlatans

Weeks to put the altars back
All to still Her sovereign hand
Though nature's planned our Fall before,
I still revere the motherland

A COCK'S CROW

A cock's crow is a reminder of firsts.
A trigger in memory, catapults a country girl
Into precious pasts and pondering.
It carries the song of dawn,
It rings in Sunday morning
I'm poring over the stove, pouring pie batters
It clangs like first bell at big school.
Where exercise books were coloured by subject.
Where I emerge freshly pressed
Into sunlight with tie knotted tight in prestige.
Where pizzas were a dollar.
Where geometry sets and graph paper
Found their way into backpacks
Before the sleep soaked rise ahead when the cock crowed.

The cock crows on behalf of this Caribbean dawn,
Though I wake up somewhere else and navigate through paler stone
And fall asleep in sprawling patchworks of green.
Where the vegetation blanket called Scotland District
Has nothing to do with the United Kingdom
Well not that they can recall anyway.
Where betrayal is part of past colonial
And crowing cocks herald colourful country sides
On this side of the Atlantic

THE BEARDED LAND

My poor memories of this place
Are numbered and few
Here was the genesis
Of a new light laden journey
After a general age of darkness
A separation from mother's breast
And a cleaving to a new land
Hued in black and blue
With golden sand
And housed in rolling beauty green
Never to be recalled again
By the mighty Queen
And her larger island.
Who knew freedom could be found,
In a land whose ground
Was watered by blood
And easily floods?
Yet reclaiming its polish and sheen
Summoning its own red, valiant queen
Refined in sun, restored in dew
With freedom fresh and pride imbued

Never to be recalled again
By the mighty Queen
And her larger island.

THE BEARDED LAND

JAMAICA, LAND WE LOVE

Here is a chance to come home again,
Live in a space I had once been in.
Here, mountains climb like steeples
Overlap as they loom over people
Tower in strength, bearing emerald bounty
Summits recalling my beautiful country
Larger than life and bigger than me
Aloud, nature sings its old, deep melody
I always look up and smile with Chronixx
The hills hold my focus, my eyes are fixed
Through dense forest, grandmother's gripping tight
The cast iron pot with all of her might
My aunt in her water boots, plants in the clear
This must be the same land my heart clutches near
I'm gripped by morning air in Moneague
Cold fingers unlocking my memory
Kingston or Kingstown, a slight difference
I settle for beautiful nuance
Here I've found myself ensconced
I am in two places at once
I am in one place twice
I am home to be precise

QUIET SPACES

Sometimes
I look for quiet spaces to write
In company of West India
In company of Majesty
In company of Me
The Ocean gushes dreamy green
Littered in auburn canopy
How can it be
That I should take
An interest in the things He makes
The bristling of the slender tree
Its leaves and boughs waving to me
The natural coursing of the air
The birds are singing of l'espere
And where do I happen to be?
Seated in majesty
Upon the emerald threads beneath
My brown, tanned legs, my sandy feet
And where do I happen to be?
Where glistening sun and eyes may meet
Upon the flat, beneath the sky
In quiet spaces there am I

AINA

Come halfway around the world
To find herself: home
In paradise again.
Escapades of breeze.
Powder bordered seas.
Just like magazines.
Very well prettied up,
To impress.

Still an island girl, from a remote place,
Looking for little more than
Bathing suits and wide brimmed hats.
Passing by palace-like tower peaks.
Windows glint not a streak,
Wound in gold, dazzling pieces.
A show.
Clear of what the eyes can see
Lies more than islands submarine

Plough through established edifices,
Earnest for earthy entrances
Never truly touching down
Until she cleaves to the land.

Leaving with no thought of Aina
Is just another smiling vacation,
Another potential exploitation,
With no appreciation,
For an island nation,
Too often obscured
By a history of colonization.

Land slid from Geronimo
From Chatoyer when the foreigners arrived
From perhaps polished Pocahontas
Who knew that Earth is most alive
When unclaimed and embraced:
Kamehameha's kingdom thrived
Far from the waves of pop culture.

So island girl sees mountains in men,
Volcanoes in resistance,
Hails hibiscus in her heart,
Not for sale like hires on the highway.
There is too much history of bloodshed
To have smiling vacations on an island
And forget about aloha Aina

Without you, how would I
Peer through kaleidoscope of cathedral glass

ENSEMBLE

ENSEMBLE

I'd once heard of a creature
With four arms and four legs
Janus faced.
Suddenly struck by pragmatic lightning
Torn at the ligaments by tongues alight
Distributed in perplexed fragments
Swallowed in temperamental squall.

I dared to put Babel together again.
Devote hope to a cleft parlance.
If I can't find Eden, I'll make it here
Sinew our hearts with holiness
Craft a mosaic of determination.
Without you, how would I
Peer through kaleidoscope of cathedral glass
And look beyond the Pieta
And know our love embodied lives?

I won't wait for buried, broken bones
To nurse tears.
I'll open my mouth
As my voice cracks
And sol-fa the truth between us
Our mouths will meet with equal full voice
In convergent symphony
A myth in a moment
Whole

CALABASH

Low and heavy
Sitting on your ovaries
Large, globular harvest
Not butterflies as they say
But still mellifluous

Tufts of dark coils
Descend like peahen fathers
Wispy, passing quicker than the months

If your orotund feet would carry you
If gunslingers won't collapse beneath the earth
Under your weight
If the sway in your circular hips could save
If you could extend the doses of short breath
Perhaps you could deliver this provision from the ground
And see your fruit
Breathe

THE RAIN CHILDREN

Deep in kumbla –
Dense, high, peridot dressed titans.
Shrubbery cascading down into narrow trenches
Silken shadows sitting on roots.
Transparent fruits hang from ossified branches
Legba summons the gathering
Shango thunders high above in tissues of purple blue
Softer than flesh
More magical, temporal
Miraculous precipitation
Water babies born from God's washed fingers
Damp with prayers from smooth faces –
Children of Africa all
With needs diverse.
Water babies nourish a cracked and thirsty surface
Carelessly in tumultuous seeds
Rolling over and tearing thatch apart
Shouting altogether as they embrace the silent soil.
And emerge as something else

TERRALECTICS

Grounding is not always penalty
Rooted in fertile volcanic wealth
Wrapped in roaring, unrelenting soil
A seed springing from noise to voice
Breaking plates through the surface
With conviction
Earth bound but clothed in erudite green
Fixed in neutral jing, possessed by bounty
Burgeoning on the outside
But always quick to look within
Standing tall with a fortified trunk
Facing the wind, unmovable
Flourishing

Notes

A Song in Asylum – *red roof* – commonly known Vincentian synecdoche for the mental institution.

Horseman, Pass by – this poem is in memory of the Barbadian woman who endured the tragedy in 2020 of losing her young twin infants while breastfeeding.

Silent Night – this poem is committed to the Heiligenthal family, especially the matriarch of the family Kalley who is popularly known as a Bethel worship leader. She lost her baby Olive near to Christmas and has openly shared and inspired with her journey of grief and Christian faith. The line "qui-la-la" is onomatopoeic in imitating a lullaby but it is also a tribute to Chris Quilala and his family. He is known for being a worship leader at Jesus Culture, who also lost his baby Jethro.

Sou Sou – a *sou sou* in the Caribbean is a method of saving money or a loan system. Each member of a group would contribute the same amount of money each month and every month a member receives the full quantity contributed by the group. If there are twelve people in the group, each person will have a chance to collect twelve times what they put in each month once in the year.

The Looking Glass – the last few lines allude to Oscar Wilde's Dorian from *The Picture of Dorian Grey*.

Hairstory – *Cascado* is a local word used to describe cornrows and pineapple braid hairstyles in St. Vincent and the Grenadines.

Mutiny – *Garinagu* is another name for the Garifuna peoples of St. Vincent and the Grenadines. This poem is a tribute to those who were banished to Baliceaux and then to Roatan Island.

Aina – *Aina* is the Hawaiian term for land, a native declaration of ownership and colonial resistance as Yurumein is the Kalinago name for St. Vincent.

Terralectics – this poem is a tribute to Kamau Brathwaite and his brilliant concept of *tidalectics* which I've put in dialogue with my own coinage *terralectics*.

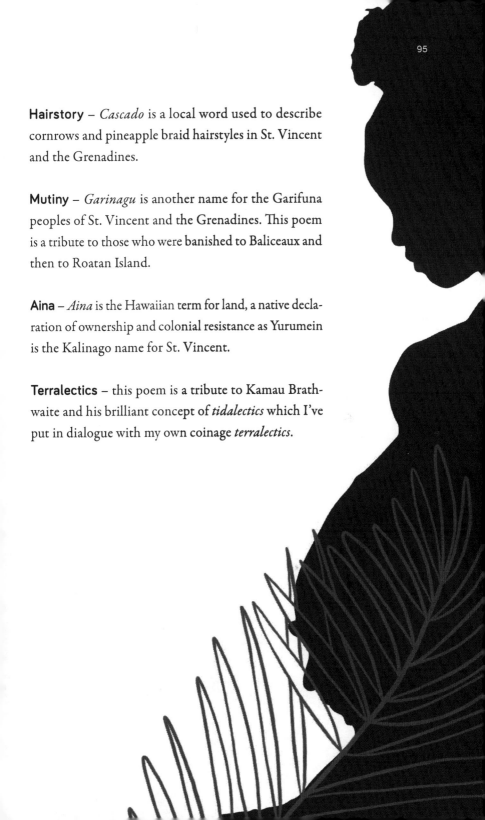

About the Author

Jacinth Howard (née Browne) holds a PhD in Literatures in English. Currently, she teaches Literature at the University of the West Indies. Her published critical work focuses on speculative fiction and can be found in JWIL, SFRA Review, Afro-Caribbean Women's Writing and Early American Literature among other works. She writes prose fiction and poetry, some of which has been published in BIM: Arts for the 21st Century, Intersect ANU, Disaster Matters, What a Year, 2021 and others. Dr Howard's creative work focuses on themes of motherhood, postcolonialism, nature and history. In 2020, she won second prize at the Frank Collymore Literary Endowment with her poetry manuscript The Mother Island. This is her first published book. Jacinth was born in St. Vincent and the Grenadines. She currently lives with her husband and two children in Barbados.

More of Jacinth's writing may be found on her blog at thelightinthecracks.com, and she would be happy to hear from you via email at jacinthisp05@gmail.com. Jacinth also has a presence on Instagram @thelightinthecracks.

Manufactured by Amazon.ca
Bolton, ON

33954211R10061